THREE SHEETS *to the* WIND

D1603828

THREE SHEETS
to the
WIND

The Nautical Origins
of Everyday Expressions

Cynthia Barrett

Illustrations by **Vail Barrett**

LP
LYONS
PRESS

Guilford, Connecticut

An imprint of The Rowman & Littlefield Publishing Group, Inc.
4501 Forbes Blvd., Ste. 200
Lanham, MD 20706
www.rowman.com

Distributed by NATIONAL BOOK NETWORK

British Library Cataloguing in Publication Information available

Library of Congress Cataloging-in-Publication Data available

ISBN 978-1-4930-4227-2 (paperback)
ISBN 978-1-4930-4228-9 (e-book)

∞™ The paper used in this publication meets the minimum requirements
of American National Standard for Information Sciences—Permanence of
Paper for Printed Library Materials, ANSI/NISO Z39.48-1992.

Printed in the United States of America

For my great-grandfather, George Washington Barrett, a whaler, who sailed around Cape Horn three times. For my father, a Navy Lieutenant who served in the D-Day Invasion of France. For my mother, who stood on the shore watching over us. And for Susi, a north star in a big sky.

The whalemen of Cold Spring Harbor, Long Island, reunite for this 1906 photograph. *From left to right:* George Washington Barrett, George Mahan, Harvey Gardiner, John Douglas, and John Waters.

Introduction

T he English language is chock-full of nautical
expressions. The earth is, after all, the water
planet. Words and phrases coined by seamen
trip off the tongue. A look at old maps shows the
cross-hatching of age-old naval and trade routes. Textiles,
spices, indigo, and other sought after goods emerged from
cargo holds. What also came ashore was the language of
sailors.

This inherited idiomatic nautical language is spoken
so often in conversation that it goes unnoticed. Filibusters
are an invention of pirates, not the US Senate, and the first
skyscrapers were the tallest sails on a ship.

Three Sheets to the Wind is an illustrated guide to your
language, so that the next time you call your friend a
"loose cannon" you know it is you who is talking like a
sailor.

THREE SHEETS *to the* WIND

A1

An insurance rating, not a steak sauce. Lloyd's of London got its start rating ships according to the quality of construction. A1 was first class.

Above Board

Pirate ships convinced passing seafarers they were no threat by concealing most of the crew below deck. In contrast, merchant ships, with nothing to hide, carried equipment and crew on deck and in plain sight. That openness is reflected in today's meaning—transparent, straightforward dealing.

> It's all open and aboveboard, apparently. After the war, Boney's Old Guard formed an organization for mutual aid. In 1816 they decided to become colonists. Your lordship must have heard something about the project?
>
> —C. S. FORESTER
> *Admiral Hornblower in the West Indies*

Adrift

A ship detached from its mooring and floating randomly with the wind, tides, or currents. A person who is dissatisfied and aimless is adrift.

Albatross

With wingspans of up to eleven feet and the ability to glide for hundreds of miles, the albatross fueled the imaginations of seafarers who believed these huge birds contained the souls of dead sailors. Killing an albatross was bad luck. Today having an albatross around one's neck is to carry a heavy, unshakeable burden.

> …what evil looks
> Had I from old and young!
> Instead of the cross, the Albatross
> About my neck was hung.
>
> —SAMUEL TAYLOR COLERIDGE
> *The Rime of the Ancient Mariner*

All Hands on Deck

During a storm or other crises, the boatswain's cry of "all hands on deck" signaled the entire crew to handle the sail. These days it is an entreaty or order for everyone to pitch in and help with a problem or reach a goal.

"It was all hands on deck then, with a rush…to get the eighteen heavy yards around with the wind howling against them the wrong way…. It was a wild scene, that, with the tropic rain falling solidly on the boys' faces as they ran about the deck, bawling their sailors' shouts…."

—ALAN VILLIERS, aboard the tall ship *Duchess*

Aloof

From the Dutch word "loef" meaning to sail into the wind. In order to safely clear the shore when a wind was blowing the ship towards this danger, the vessel pointed into the wind and away from the hazard. This nautical technique for maintaining distance inspired its figurative meaning of being emotionally distant or indifferent.

With all our force we kept aloof to sea, and gain'd the island where our vessel lay.

—HOMER
The Odyssey

Around the Horn

——— ⚓ ———

Before the Panama Canal, ships had to navigate around Cape Horn, the southernmost part of South America, to sail between the Atlantic and Pacific Oceans. Around the horn now commonly describes the baseball ritual of infielders throwing the ball around the bases after a strike out and with no runners on.

> The decks were covered with snow, and there was a constant driving of sleet. In fact, Cape Horn had set in with good earnest. In the midst of all this, and before it became dark, we had all the studding-sails to make up and stow away, and then to lay aloft and rig in all the booms, for and aft, and coil away the tacks, sheets, and halyards. This was pretty tough work for four or five hands, in the face of the gale which almost took us off the yards, and with ropes so stiff with ice that it was almost impossible to bend them.
>
> —RICHARD HENRY DANA JR.
> *Two Years Before the Mast*

Arrive

To arrive literally meant to reach land after a voyage at sea. The word comes from the Latin "arripare," meaning to touch the shore.

Arsenal

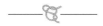

Arsenal comes from the Italian "arzenale," meaning wharf. It originally described Venice's massive waterfront. By the 1500s, London and other major seaports adopted the word for their harbors. Only later did arsenal take on its meaning as a secured storehouse for munitions and military equipment.

As the Crow Flies

When lost in coastal waters, sailors shimmied up the ship's mast and released a crow from a cage. The crow flew straight toward the nearest shore. The lookout platform at the top of the mast was called the "crow's nest." The expression "as the crow flies" implies the most direct route.

At Loggerheads

In order to caulk the seams of the ship's deck, tar was melted using a long rod with a solid hot iron ball at one end. The repair work was a nasty and tiresome business, and when tempers flared the loggerheads became convenient weapons for the crew. The expression still suggests a hot-tempered disagreement.

They had been sparring, in the spirit of fun, with loggerheads, those massy iron balls with long handles to be carried red-hot from the fire and plunged into buckets of tar or pitch so that the substance might be melted with no risk of flame.

—Patrick O'Brian
The Commodore

At Loose Ends

——— ⋈ ———

During periods of relative calm, idle sailors were ordered to repair and splice the frayed ends of lines. Those assigned this tedious task were described as being at loose ends. Now the phrase means not knowing what to do with one's self.

Back and Fill

When maneuvering in tight areas such as crowded harbors or narrow channels a ship had to slow down and hold its position. To do so it alternately filled or spilled wind from the sails. A person who equivocates may be said to hem and haw or back and fill.

> She backs and fills; the sails slat and fill again; the sea gurgles round cutwater and stern with that sickening bath-draining sound that tells of stayed progress.
>
> — ALAN VILLIERS
> *Voyage of the Parma*

Bail Out

To bail out is to scoop water from a swamped or leaking boat. From Old French "bail," a small wooden bucket. The expression now describes extricating oneself from a bad predicament.

> Inside the bunkhouse things were a mess. We have about six inches of water in the room. We bail and bail, but every sea higher than the door board lets in more gallons of water.
>
> —RAY WILMORE,
> aboard the four masted barque *John Ena*

Ballast

Ships with no paying cargo filled their empty holds with stones or other heavy objects to create stability and balance. They were said to be sailing "in ballast," from the Old English "bar," to be bare, and "hladan," to load. Today ballast also means to support by showing good character and morals. King George VI remained at Buckingham Palace during the bombing of the city to ballast Londoners.

> The handiest ballast was stone, but sometimes pig iron or pig lead could be carried as part of the cargo.
>
> —ALEXANDER LAING
> *Clipper Ship Men*

Bamboozle

Before it took on its nautical meaning, to be bamboozled was to make someone look as foolish as a baboon. British seamen were bamboozled by the ruse of enemy Spanish warships flying the flag of a friendly nation. These days it means to con someone by clever, underhanded methods.

Batten Down the Hatches

Colloquially, to prepare for trouble. Batten comes from Old French "baston," meaning a stick or flat strip of wood. In foul weather, the crew stretched tarpaulins over the hatches and pinned down the edges with the battens.

The hatches were constantly battened down, and when the forward deck began to leak, Bligh gave orders that people should sling their hammocks in the great cabin aft.

—CHARLES NORDHOFF AND JAMES NORMAN HALL
Mutiny on the Bounty

Bedlam

A corruption of the name of the Bethlehem Hospital, London's oldest and most infamous psychiatric institution. Naval seamen who were unhinged as a result of cannon shelling, isolation, or alcohol were sent by the British Admiralty to this institution, and made up a solid percentage of its patients. Once committed, sailors were subject to Bethlehem's vicious practices. Londoners paid a penny to gawk at these "lunatics" shackled to their beds. Over time these "Penny visitors" used the word bedlam to describe noisy chaos.

Bell Bottoms

Bell bottoms were a signature mark of a sailor's uniform. Invented by mariners, these dark blue serge trousers flared out to a wide bell shape below the knee, making it easy to roll the pant leg above the knees when swabbing the deck. Surplus navy bell bottoms became an icon of 1960s fashion—but with the added flourish of embroidered peace signs and flowers.

Between the Devil and the Deep Blue Sea

The "devil" was the topmost plank of the ship's side closest to the deck. Caulking this long seam in the tight space was a grueling task. One false move and a sailor could find himself plunging into the water. Today someone between the devil and the deep blue sea is in a lousy situation with no good options.

Bitter End

The in-board end of a ship's anchor cable was secured to a sturdy wooden or iron deck post called the "bitts." In deep waters when the anchor line was completely played out, it reached the bitter end. It could go no further.

Blacklist

A black list contained the names of sailors being reprimanded or punished. It is probably derived from "black books" which were codifications of the laws, customs, and practices of the sea. Vessels violating these books were vulnerable to sanction in foreign ports. The word blacklist still conveys a similar meaning. It is a record of persons under suspicion or targeted for punishment.

Blazer

To add color and flash to naval ceremonies, British captains used their own money to purchase uniforms for the crew. Captain John Washington of the *Blazer* chose a striking blue and white uniform. Originally his crew was known as "The Blazers." Eventually the popular jacket was called a blazer.

Blood Money

The British Admiralty offered a financial reward for destroying enemy ships. The bounty paid was based on the number of crew killed. The phrase has taken on the broader meaning of money for murder.

Blowhard

Sailors likened a boastful crewmate to an incessant, loud wind. A blowhard is full of bluster but no substance.

Blue Monday

Punishment for a sailor's misdeed was meted out on Mondays. The men dreaded Mondays as the day of reckoning. Because it is the beginning of our workweek, Monday remains an unpopular day.

> ...petty pillferings and commissiones of that kinde, those were generallie punished with the whippe...and commonlie this execution is done upon Mondaye morninges...
>
> —"Punishment of Seamen in the Reign of Queen Elizabeth"

Bolster

Smooth blocks of wood, often wrapped in canvas, were fitted into the rigging to prevent chaffing against hard or rough edges of the mast or other parts of the ship. These days it means to strengthen or support something or someone.

Boot Camp

During the Spanish-American War, navy recruits wore leggings called boots. These newly enlisted sailors trained in "boot" camps. In everyday life boot camp now describes a tough, intense program of self-improvement.

Bootlegger

Originally bootleggers were sailors who smuggled ashore bottles of liquor hidden in their large sea boots. The term gained popularity in the 1920s during Prohibition when people smuggling alcohol were called bootleggers.

By and Large

A ship sailing "by the wind" is heading into the wind just enough so that the sail stays full. To sail "large" is to sail with the sails out at an angle to the boat, requiring fewer adjustments of the sail. "By and large" is to alternate between the two. Although the boat's course is less direct, it gets there. The phrase is now used to characterize something broadly.

Careen

Careening is the technique of sharply tilting a ship so that the hull is exposed for caulking, painting, and other repairs. From Old French "careen," meaning the keel of a ship. These days the word describes swaying, out-of-control, rapid forward movement. Gus the bulldog careened down the hill on a skateboard.

Carry On

In a strong, favorable wind, a command was given to hoist all the canvas sail the rigging could handle. The sails were "on" to maximize headway. The popular British slogan "keep calm and carry on," coined during World War II, means to remain unruffled and progress.

> The wind was now due south-west, and blowing a gale to which a vessel close hauled could have shown no more than a single close-reefed sail; but as we were going before it, we could carry on.

—RICHARD HENRY DANA JR.
Two Years Before the Mast

Cartel

A negotiation between hostile navies regarding the exchange of prisoners was called a cartel. The word came to be applied to the go-between ship, flying a white truce flag, which carried out negotiations. The agreement was often in writing, hence the Latin derivation "carta," or card. In today's world, a cartel is a pact (often illegal) to control prices, production, and competition.

Dear Sir

I received your letter of the 9th. Instant with a Copy of the Letter from the Admiralty Office relative to the proposed Exchange of Prisoners, in which the precise Number of those we have here is desired…If the number we have falls short of the 250, the Cartel ship may take back as many of those she brings….

—BENJAMIN FRANKLIN TO DAVID HARTLEY
October 20, 1778

Castaway

A shipwrecked sailor marooned on an isolated shore. The most famous castaway in literature is in Daniel Defoe's 1719 novel *Robinson Crusoe*.

Catwalk

A narrow protected passageway on a ship, catwalks are used by sailors when moving about in foul weather. Catwalks date back to the age of square-riggers and are still found on tankers and other modern-day vessels. Nowadays the word conjures up fashion shows and supermodels.

Caulk-Off

To caulk-off means to take a nap. Tar used to caulk the ship's deck seams softened in the sun. When a sailor snuck in a mid-day snooze, the deck left telltale streaks on his clothing.

When the calking was finished, two coats of copper paint were slapped on the bottom, two of white lead on the topsides and bulwarks.

—Joshua Slocum
Sailing Alone Around the World

Chew the Fat

Salt-cured meat was a staple on long sea voyages. While chewing the tough briny beef, sailors exchanged stories and chewed the fat. Similarly, when we chew the fat we are exchanging friendly banter and gossip.

Chit

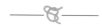

Chits were vouchers or notes used by seamen for onboard goods or services. The word was first introduced by sailors of the Dutch East India Company, and later adopted by British crews. It comes from the Hindi word "chitthi," letter or note, and Sanskrit "chitras," picture or sketch. Nowadays a chit is an informal written IOU.

Chockablock

In order to sail fast upwind, a piece of wood, known as a chock, from Old French "coche," was wedged into the pulley, or block. The pulleys were tight up against each other such that pulling on the line allowed no further movement or increase of speed. On New Year's Eve, Times Square is chockablock with revelers.

Clean Bill of Health

A clean bill of health was literally a document issued by a port authority certifying that at the time of sailing, no one at the port and none of the ship's crew was infected with cholera, the plague, or other contagious diseases. The certificate had to be presented at the next port of call before permission to dock was granted.

Clean Slate

Headings, distances, tacks, and speed were recorded on a slate kept by the helmsman. At the end of each watch the entries were transferred to the ship's log, and the slate was wiped clean for use on the next watch. The phrase now means to get a fresh start.

Clean Sweep

A clean sweep is an overpowering surf that washes away everything on deck. The origin of the phrase dates to the Dutch Admiral Maarten Tromp's crushing defeat of the British in the 1652 Battle of Dungeness. Admiral Tromp fixed a broom to the masthead, signaling to all that he had swept the British from the seas.

Clear the Decks

In preparation for action the decks of warships were cleared of all non-essentials. This prevented fires and allowed the crew to move quickly amidst the smoke and chaos of battle.

> Say you go on board a line-of-battle ship: you see everything scrupulously neat; you see all the decks clear and unobstructed as the sidewalks of Wall Street of a Sunday morning....
>
> —HERMAN MELVILLE
> *White-Jacket*

Close Quarters

—— ✠ ——

As protection against pirates, sailors on merchant ships erected wooden fort-like barricades on the quarterdeck. When under attack, the crew crowded shoulder to shoulder inside the fortification and fired their muskets through the small holes carved in the timbers. In his 1769 book, *An Universal Dictionary of the Marine*, William Falconer describes "…an English merchant ship, of fifteen guns, and properly fitted with close-quarters, defeat the united efforts of three French privateers who boarded her…"

Coast Is Clear

The call "coast is clear" signaled to law abiding ships that the vessel was safely past a hazardous shore. For smugglers it indicated no risk ahead of detection by customs officials or law enforcement agents.

Cold Enough to Freeze the Balls off a Brass Monkey

To speed reloading, cannon balls were stacked on deck in a pyramid and secured with a brass gizmo called a "monkey." The monkey had one critical flaw. Bitter cold temperatures caused the brass to contract and pop out the balls.

Cup of Joe

The days of rum, beer, and officers' personal wine supply dried up with the appointment of Josephus Daniels as Secretary of the Navy. In 1914 this stern Methodist and prohibitionist banned "…the use or introduction for drinking purposes of alcoholic liquors on board any naval vessel, or within any navy yard or station." As a substitute, stewards increased orders for coffee. Naval lore has it that the disgruntled sailors tagged the poor substitute "cup of Josephus Daniels," and later the shorter "cup of Joe."

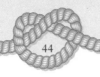

Cut and Run

For quick escape, a captain ordered his crew to cut the anchor line and lashings of furled sails, to hastily run with the wind. This maneuver was only acceptable under dire circumstances since a lost anchor and damaged rigging was costly. Figuratively it means to swiftly abandon a bad situation.

"What? Jack, my great man of the main-top, gone!" cried the Captain: "I'll not believe it."
"Jack Chase cut and run!" cried a sentimental middy. "It must have been all for love, then; the signoritas have turned his head."

—HERMAN MELVILLE
White-Jacket

Cut of His Jib

Sailors observed the distinct shape, height, and size of the jib sail to determine if an approaching ship was from a friendly or hostile nation. Since warships were masters of deception, this method of identification was far from reliable. The expression now means to form an opinion of someone based solely on his or her appearance.

The well preserved man of no little stamina, if a trife prone to baldness, there was something spurious in the cut of his jib that suggested a jail delivery.

— JAMES JOYCE
Ulysses

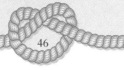

Dead in the Water

A windless day is the bane of all sailors. With no breeze to fill the sails, a ship is inert and lifeless. The crew perceived their motionless vessel as being dead in the water. Superstitious mariners believed they could stir the winds by whistling and sticking a knife in the mast. The blade and handle of the knife formed a crucifix—suggesting it held supernatural religious powers. The phrase now means a proposal or plan with zero chance of success.

Dead Weight

A ship's dead weight is the difference between an empty ship and when it is fully loaded. In a group effort, a person who contributes nothing is a dead weight.

Dead Wood

Wood attached to the keel as filler between structural elements of the ship added no strength to the hull. Nowadays it generally refers to people institutions clear out because they underperform or don't add to the bottom line. In *The Shadow-Line*, Joseph Conrad describes the perception of parts of a ship being dead:

> That illusion of life and character which charms one in men's finest handiwork radiated from her. An enormous bulk of teak-wood timber swung over her hatchway: lifeless matter, looking heavier and bigger than anything aboard of her.

Debacle

The word debacle stems from the Old French "debacler," meaning to release or free. The melting of ice on a frozen river sometimes produced destructive flooding called a debacle. As a result, the word carries the negative connotation of a complete collapse or resounding failure.

Deep Six

To measure the depth of water, a weighted line was dropped overboard. The line was marked in fathoms. Each fathom equaled six feet. The sailor's cry of "deep six" meant that the ship was in six fathoms or 36 feet of water. Anything that fell off a ship in waters this deep was gone for good. To deep six something is to get rid of it forever.

Deliver a Broadside

Cannons were fixed along the broadsides of the great warships. When the enemy was within range an order was given to fire all guns simultaneously. This coordinated volley became known as a broadside. Nowadays to deliver a broadside is to hurl a crushing invective.

> The roar of broadside coincided exactly with that of Natividad's. The ship was enveloped in smoke, through which could be heard the rattling of splinters, the sound of cut rigging tumbling to the deck….

—C. S. FORESTER
Beat to Quarters

Dingbat

Dingbat was a sailor's slang name for the deck mop made out of used rope ends. When swabbing the ship, the teased out ends of the mop would fly about uncontrollably. Today dingbat is slang for an idiotic, empty-headed person.

Ditty Bag

The ditty bag was a small canvas sack containing a sailor's tools, sewing supplies, and personal articles such as letters and photos. Sailors often referred to the bag as the "housewife" because it also held domestic items such as thimbles, thread, and needles. We still use ditty bags, but inside you'll now find small, personal travel toiletries.

Don't Give Up the Ship

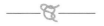

It was one of the shortest and bloodiest frigate actions of the War of 1812. James Lawrence, captain of the *Chesapeake*, fought the British ship *Shannon* off Boston Harbor in June of 1813. Within 15 minutes over 200 men were killed or wounded. The vast majority of casualties were the Americans, including 31-year-old Lawrence. Mortally wounded but still in his full-dress uniform, he issued his famous final command: "Don't give up the ship." Despite the futility of his last order, it became one of most iconic slogans of the US Navy. Eventually it came ashore as an all-purpose rallying cry.

Dressing Down

———⧈———

Worn and thin sails were treated with oil or wax to renew their strength. A process called dressing down, it was a tedious job that could be doled out as punishment. To get a dressing down today is to be subjected to a harsh reprimand.

Byam, do you know that I am a double-dyed villain? I stole one of Mr. Bligh's missing coconuts.

So it's you we have to thank for our dressing-down, you little rascal, I replied.

—CHARLES NORDHOFF and JAMES NORMAN HALL
Mutiny on the Bounty

Duffel

— ✕ —

Originating in Duffel, Belgium, this rough woolen water-resistant fabric became synonymous with a sailor's clothing and the woolen bag in which he stowed his personal effects.

I threw mes affaires hastily together (including some minor accessories which I was going to leave behind; but which t-d bade me to include) and emerged with a duffle-bag under one arm and a bed-roll under the other...

—E. E. Cummings
The Enormous Room

Dungarees

Before navies issued official uniforms, sailors often made their own work cloths. Old, discarded sails provided them with a durable fabric for pants. The name dungaree came from the Hindi word "dungri," meaning cotton cloth. These precursors to today's jeans were not blue but tan— the color of the sails from which they were cut.

Taffy Jones who washed the clothes of other men besides his own for tobacco, was usually seen in front of his washtub, or perhaps scubbing a pair of dungaree pants laid flat on the deck.

—Captain A. A. Bestic
Kicking Canvas

Even Keel

The phrase even keel describes a ship that is level and balanced with its keel perpendicular to the surface of the water. Figuratively it has come to mean a calm, stable state of mind. The opposite is to keel over meaning to capsize. Today an upright person who falls over unconscious recalls the original usage by sailors when to keel over was a synonym for to die.

Every Man for Himself

———— 🪢 ————

The order "every man for himself" was given to the crew when it was clear that the ship was sinking and beyond salvage. Today it is used in a pessimistic context.

Fathom

———— 🪢 ————

A fathom equals roughly six feet. This nautical unit of measurement is based on the span of a man's outstretched arms. The word comes from the Old English "faedem," to embrace. Sailors measured ocean depths, anchor chains, ropes, and cables in fathoms. Although marines eventually abandoned fathoms for meters, we onshore still reach for the word fathom to express our ability to comprehend, grasp, or get to the bottom of things.

> We...let the wind and steersman work the ship with full sail spread all day above our coursing, till the sun dipped, and all the ways grew dark upon the fathomless unresting sea.
>
> —Homer
> *The Odyssey*

Feeling Blue

When an officer died during a voyage, sailors painted a blue band around the hull and raised a blue flag for the return passage to home. Henry Newbolt's poem "The Quarter-Gunner's Yarn" depicts the scene after the death of Admiral Lord Nelson during the Battle of Trafalgar: "Then we hauled down the flag, at the fore it was red, and blue at the mizzen was hoisted instead…."

Figurehead

Figureheads are carved wooden figures affixed to the ship's bow. Since Ancient Egypt, mariners have considered ships living things. They created figureheads to imbue their vessels with special powers. A carved bird provided eyes to guide the ship, a lion courage, and a saint divine intervention. In the 1800s the long, sleek clipper ships adopted a full-length human figure. Some of these depicted men, but the majority were beautiful, scantily clad women that pleased both the sea gods and the crew. Today a figurehead is an apparent leader with high visibility but only nominal power and authority.

Filibuster

Filibusters were pirates off the coast of the Caribbean Spanish American territories. The word made its way into the English language from the Dutch "vrijbuiter," and Spanish "filibustero." This description of obstructive sea tactics is now applied to legislative maneuvering, most often senators speaking at length to delay or prevent a vote.

First Rate

British warships were classified according to the number of carriage-mounted guns they carried. The highest ranked ships carried one hundred or more guns on three decks. These were called first rate ships. A second rate ship was also a three-decker and had 90 to 98 guns.

> Toward the end of November I joined the Bounty at Spithead....Our ship looked no bigger than a longboat among the tall first-rates and seventy-fours at anchor near by.

> —CHARLES NORDHOFF AND JAMES NORMAN HALL
> *Mutiny on the Bounty*

Flog a Dead Horse

When a sailor signed onto a voyage it was customary to advance to him the first month's pay. The cash was often spent before embarking on the trip. After running through the money, the seaman's motivation to work hard was gone. Ship's officers found that getting men to perform extra duties was as futile as flogging a dead horse. The phrase has come to mean wasting time and energy on a hopeless matter.

Flotsam and Jetsam

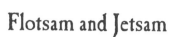

According to British law, flotsam, from Old French "floter," to float, refers to goods or wreckage accidentally lost at sea that remain floating. Jetsam is goods or parts of a vessel which sink after being deliberately jettisoned to lighten the ship. In the case of jetsam, the owner has not renounced his property and can later reclaim it. But with flotsam, it is finders keepers.

Fly-by-Night

A large sail used for light, downwind sailing. Unlike smaller light wind sails, the fly-by-night was relatively easy to manage and so was often used at night when there were few hands on deck. The phrase now suggests a business operation that is shady and likely to go bust.

Footloose

When the foot (bottom edge) of a sail is not stretched and secured along the boom, the sail is footloose, difficult to control, and dances wildly in the wind. Restraining it takes a sailor's strength and concentration—and he's feeling anything but footloose and fancy-free.

Gadget

Gadget is a catchall word for any small device or mechanical thing with an unknown or forgotten name. It is most likely from the French "gachette," meaning lock mechanism, or from "gage," meaning tool. In his 1886 book, *Spunyard and Spindrift*, Robert Brown describes how when sailors can't remember the name of something "…they call it a chicken-fixing, or a gadjet, or a gill-guy, or a timmy-noggy, or a wim-wam…"

Garbled

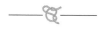

Garble was the prohibited practice of combining rubbish with the ship's cargo. Violators were subject to stiff fines, and if garbage was found mixed with foodstuffs permission to unload was denied. The word has come to describe messages that are so distorted and mixed up that they are indecipherable.

Get Cracking

To avoid penalties for late delivery, mail ships often carried the maximum amount of sail and set the rigging so tautly that the sails made a cracking noise under the tension.

Get Down to Brass Tacks

———— ⊷⊶ ————

To get down to brass tacks is to quit dithering and attack the business at hand. The most likely origin of this expression is traced to the high seas. Ships used brass fittings rather than iron because brass does not corrode. A sailor had to get down to brass tacks and focus on the work of polishing the metalwork to a high sheen.

A fine flibbertigibbet you are," said Hurst. "Look at that brass-work! D'you call that bright? Where d'you keep your eyes? What's your division been doing this last hour?

—C. S. Forester
Commodore Hornblower

Gets the Point

After reaching a verdict in the court-martial of a British officer, a sword was laid on a table in front of the accused. If the point was towards him, he'd been found guilty; if the handle was towards him, he'd been found innocent.

Give a Wide Berth

For safety and maneuverability, ships need plenty of sea room. The term "berth" comes from the practice of "bearing off"—steering away from an oncoming ship, or natural hazard like a rocky shoal. Ships at anchor also require a generous amount of space since winds, tides, and currents shift its position. The phrase nowadays means to deliberately avoid or keep one's distance.

There in the middle of the moonlit valley below them stood the "ha'nted" house, utterly isolated… the boys gazed awhile…they struck far off to the right, to give the haunted house a wide berth, and took their way homeward through the woods….

—MARK TWAIN
The Adventures of Tom Sawyer

Glad Rags

Sailors changed into their best attire when going on shore leave. From Old English "glaed" meaning bright, shining. Shirley Temple, wearing bows and fancy clothes, captured America's heart in the 1933 movie *From Glad Rags to Riches*.

Go by the Board

—— ⋈ ——

"Bord" is the Anglo-Saxon name for the side of a ship. Anything that blew or slid off the ship's side while it was underway was gone for good. When something goes by the board it is rejected or abandoned.

> Her rattling shrouds, all sheathed in ice,
> With the masts went by the board;
> Like a vessel of glass, she stove and sank,
> Ho! ho! the breakers roared.

—HENRY WADSWORTH LONGFELLOW
The Wreck of the Hesperus

Grapple

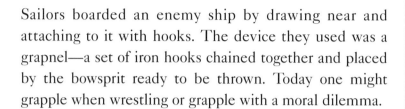

Sailors boarded an enemy ship by drawing near and attaching to it with hooks. The device they used was a grapnel—a set of iron hooks chained together and placed by the bowsprit ready to be thrown. Today one might grapple when wrestling or grapple with a moral dilemma.

Groggy

To keep sailors sober and in fighting form, the 18th century British admiral Edward Vernon ordered that rum rations be diluted with water. This thinned drink became known as grog. Vernon was nicknamed "Old Grog" because his navy cloak was made of a rough grogram fabric. Even at the prescribed one part rum, three parts water, it could make sailors very groggy.

Groundswell

Deep ocean waves grow larger as they move over uneven seabeds and are felt as surface undulations. Colloquially, the term describes a widespread surge of public opinion.

Sea of stretched ground-swells!
Sea breathing broad and convulsive breaths!
Sea of the brine of life!
Sea of unshovelled and always-ready graves!

—WALT WHITMAN
Leaves of Grass

Half-Mast

As a symbolic gesture of mourning, sailors slackened rigging, allowed sails to luff, and lowered flags to give the ship a drooping, downcast appearance. A flag flown at half-mast is a tribute to the deceased.

Hand over Fist

Agile sailors could rapidly swarm up a ship's rigging. One hand gripped the line in a fist while the other hand reached above for the next line. The expression now means to accomplish something swiftly.

Happy Hour

In 1913 the crew of the USS *Arkansas* began holding afternoon gatherings that included boxing, smoking, music, and talkies. By the 1920s much of the US Navy was throwing these morale-boosting parties.

Hard and Fast

A ship that is firmly beached on land is said to be hard and fast. The phrase is now used figuratively to describe an inflexible and rigid opinion or rule.

> …the ship struck and stuck fast. Immediately upon this we took in all our sails, hoisted out the boats and sounded round the ship, and found that we had got upon the south-east edge of a reef of coral rocks…
>
> —CAPTAIN JAMES COOK
> *Journal During the First Voyage Round the World*

High and Dry

For a ship to run aground in a receding tide is to be left high and dry. Getting stuck with the check when everyone else has taken off is also to be left high and dry.

Hit Rock Bottom

A ship in shallow water may founder on the seabed. Encountering serious self-inflicted or unforeseen obstacles may result in dire circumstances such that the person is said to have hit rock bottom.

Hunky-Dory

Hunky Dory is the name of David Bowie's 1971 best selling album. But what is the origin of the expression? Maritime etymology traces it to the mid-1800s and the opening of trade with Japan. Sailors on leave in the harbor city of Yokohama discovered a street called "Honchi-dori" that catered to their various wants. The term has come to mean when things are not just fine but extremely satisfactory.

In the Doldrums

Sailors dreaded being becalmed in the notorious belt of low-pressure that extends five degrees above and below the equator. In this windless corridor vessels could be stuck for days, even weeks, baking in the fierce equatorial sun. The phrase now describes a listless, apathetic state of mind.

> In these doldrums we are finding more than ever the extreme boredom of our long isolation. After all, we are no more than high-spirited youngsters, and it is becoming increasingly difficult for us to grin and bare it.
>
> —KEN ATTIWILL, aboard the tall ship *Archibald Russell*

In the Offing

The offing is the area of sea between coastal waters and the horizon. Approaching ships that can be spotted from shore within these two points are said to be in the offing, about to reach port or drop anchor. The phrase is now used figuratively to describe something about to happen.

> …there were no less than four lighthouses kept flaming every night….all of which are to direct the sailors to keep a good offing in case of bad weather…
>
> —Daniel Defoe
> *Tour Through the Eastern Counties of England*

It's an Ill Wind That Blows No Good

This philosophical expression holds the same meaning today as it did for the mariners who coined the phrase centuries ago. While sailors might curse an unfavorable wind, they realize that it is a boon to seafarers navigating a different route. Though circumstances may be unfortunate for some, rarely do they benefit no one. What's bad for you may be good for others.

FALSTAFF: What wind blew you hither, Pistol?"
PISTOL: Not the ill wind which blows no man to good. Sweet knight, thou art now one of the greatest men in this realm.

—WILLIAM SHAKESPEARE
Henry IV, Part 2

Junk

Mariners referred to worn-out rigging as "junk." The word was adopted from Latin "juncus," meaning to join, which described the attaching of reeds to create rope. When lines aged, the crew's task was to tease them apart and cut them into small pieces to be reused for caulking. Bags filled with junk became fenders placed on the sides of ships to prevent damage. Later all kinds of old ship refuse was labeled as junk.

Jury-Rig

Possibly from Old French "ajure," meaning help or relief. On long voyages the crew often had to perform makeshift repairs of masts, yards, or rigging. The expression is still used to describe stopgap measures.

> …all the boats came together for the last time. I had no mast or sail in mine, but I made a mast out of a spare oar and hoisted a boat-awning for a sail, with a boat hook for a yard…
> 'Be careful with that jury-rig, Marlow,' said the captain…

—JOSEPH CONRAD
Youth: A Narrative

Keep Your Shirt On

———— ✄ ————

Masters of psychological warfare, Vikings often tore off their shirts of mail in the heat of battle. They went berserk meaning "bare-sark." "Sark" is Norse for shirt. The sight of these fierce, half-naked warriors was terrifying to their adversaries. Nowadays, to keep your shirt on means to stay calm and in control.

Knock Off

Oarsmen propelled ancient galleys. In order to keep a precise rhythm a man in the stern would strike a drum or knock on a block with a wooden mallet. When the knocking stopped, the rowers switched from leaning into their oars to leaning off them and resting. It was time to knock off.

Know the Ropes

Tall ships had miles of rigging. Each line had its own function, and it was critical for sailors to correctly identify each one. Securing or unlashing the wrong line could be catastrophic. To minimize confusion, ships tried to standardize where lines were secured on deck. To be well versed and familiar is to know the ropes.

Launch

The word launch is derived from the Old French "lanceare," meaning to pierce. To launch a boat is to slide it into the water thereby slicing into the water's surface.

> We bore down on the ship at the sea's edge
> and launched her on the salt immortal sea,
> stepping our mast and spar in the black ship...."

—HOMER
The Odyssey

Leading Light

———— ✕ ————

Two fixed beacons placed at the entrance of a harbor guided ships past rocks, reefs, shoals, and other dangers. These lights were distinguished from each other by color, distance, and height. When aligned by inbound or outbound ships they provided accurate bearings for safe passage. The phrase has come to describe an important or prominent person in a group or cause.

Leeway

A blowing wind hits and pushes on the "windward" side of a ship. The other side of the ship is the protected or "lee" side of the ship. The word leeway is from Old English "lee," meaning protection. Land on the lee side of the ship must be avoided as the wind pushes the ship into this danger. Good sailors allow plenty of leeway between the ship and the coast. Best to give grouchy people leeway.

[Queequeg] added, that he shuddered at the thought of being buried in his hammock, according to the usual sea-custom, tossed like something vile to the death devouring sharks. No: he desired a canoe like those of Nantucket, all the more congenial to him, being a whaleman, that like a whale-boat these coffin-canoes were without a keel; though that involved but uncertain steering, and much lee-way adown the dim ages.

—HERMAN MELVILLE
Moby Dick

Let the Cat Out of the Bag

A whip composed of nine pieces of cord with three knots at the striking end, the cat-o'-nine-tails was one of the authorized instruments of punishment in the British Navy until 1881. It was kept in a cloth bag. A sailor who reported the misdeeds of another let the cat out of the bag.

Lifeline

Lifeline is a rope stretched along the deck of a ship for sailors to grab onto while working in heavy weather.

Listless

In a stiff breeze, sailboats heel (list) sharply to starboard or port. In light winds, a boat loosens its list and moves sluggishly on an even keel. The word has come to describe a languid, indifferent person.

Log Book

—⚓—

Ships kept daily records on speed, distance, sightings, and various incidents. The name log book reflects the technique used for determining speed. A wedge of wood attached to a line was tossed overboard. Speed was calculated based on the amount of line that played out within a certain time. The word log is still synonymous with keeping a running record.

The mate went below, and presently emerged with a hand log and sandglass. He handed the sandglass to me....The moment the sand ran out the boy sang out "Stop!" and the men grabbed the line, holding it while the Mate noted, by the nearest mark, what speed the vessel was doing.

— SIR JAMES BISSET
Sail Ho!

Long Shot

The crude, heavy naval cannon introduced in the time of Henry VIII seldom hit a target that was far off. Because a long shot that found its mark was rare, a ship had to draw close to the enemy before firing its guns. For us, winning the lottery is a long shot.

Loose Cannon

In heavy weather, when a cannon broke away from the mount it rolled uncontrollably around the deck, injuring crew members and damaging everything in its path. Someone who talks or acts impulsively and causes trouble may be called a loose cannon.

> Something terrible had just happened. One of the cannonades of the battery, a twenty-four pounder, had broken loose. This is the most dangerous accident that can possibly take place on shipboard….A cannon that breaks its moorings suddenly becomes some strange supernatural beast.
>
> —Victor Hugo
> *Ninety-Three*

Lower the Boom

The boom is the long horizontal pole that controls the movement of the sail. It can deliver sailors a knockout blow if it swings wildly or collapses in heavy weather. These days the phrase means to put a stop to, chastise, or rebuke.

Mainstay

The mainstay is a strong line that is central to the stability of the main mast and the word equates with critical support. Like an onboard fire or loose cannon, a snapped mainstay was a catastrophic event on a ship.

The great sail bellied out horizontally as though it would lift up the main stay; the blocks rattled and flew about…

—RICHARD HENRY DANA, JR.
Two Years Before the Mast

Make a Toast

The phrase make a toast traces back to the old waterfront alehouses where a popular drink among sailors was a small piece of toast placed in a mulled wine or hot toddy.

Mind Your P's and Q's

Ironically, this admonishment to be on one's best behavior is rooted in the rough and tumble world of alehouses. Sailors favored tavern keepers who offered credit. Mindful about keeping these tabs accurate, owners wrote the names of each customer on a board, and next to it the number of "P's" (pints) and "Q's" (quarts) drunk. Owners made sure each sailor paid up on payday.

Miss the Boat

This expression referred to sailors who missed the ride ferrying them from shore leave back to the ship. Colloquially it describes blowing an opportunity.

Miss the Mark

Sailboats competing in a regatta must pass or round a specified side of a buoy, the mark, before going onto the next leg of the course. A boat that misses the mark must go back and round it correctly before advancing. The expression has taken on the broader meaning of failing to achieve one's aim.

Monkey Jacket

———— ✕ ————

The monkey jacket was a close-fitting, short navy coat. The practical design made it popular with sailors because it freed up their legs for climbing the rigging. The jacket got its nickname from its similarity to the little coat worn by the organ grinder's monkey. Because tuxedos have a similar close fit, they also have been tagged as monkey jackets.

> He complained of a pain in his breast and said he was cold, although buttoned up with a monkey jacket on.
>
> —MARTHA SMITH BREWER BROWN,
> aboard the whaling ship *Lucy Ann*

Moonlighting

To avoid detection, smugglers came ashore at night to off-load their contraband. The expression has lost its surreptitious meaning and now describes working a second job.

Navy Blue

British Naval officers petitioned the Admiralty for a standard uniform in 1748. The proposals for the regulation dress varied in style and colors, including the national colors blue and red. King George II chose dark blue with contrasting white facing. He said his choice was inspired by the sight of the Duchess of Bedford on horseback in Hyde Park wearing a riding habit in those colors. As navies around the world adopted similar dark blue uniforms, the color became known as navy blue.

No Great Shakes

To save deck space, empty wooden casks were "shaken" (taken apart) so the pieces, called shakes, could be compactly stowed. Eventually these shakes might be sold, but only at a very low price. The expression is now used to dismiss someone or something as mediocre, unexceptional, and of little value.

Oil on Troubled Waters

To allow for maneuvering in stormy seas, sailors resorted to the practice of pouring oil overboard. The oil spread across a surprisingly large area. This thin layer increased the water surface tension, diminishing the ocean chop. The phrase has come to describe someone who diffuses a tense situation.

I remained in Gloucester about two weeks, fitting out with the various articles for the voyage most readily obtained there. The owners of the wharf where I lay, and of the many fishing-vessels, put on board dry cod galore, also a barrel of oil to calm the waves.

—Joshua Slocum
Sailing Alone Around the World

On Deck

—— ⊗ ——

To be on deck, rather than below decks, signified that a sailor was ready and able to execute orders. The command "all hands on deck" addressed the entire ship's company: crew and officers.

> This was a well-drilled crew; the ship was working like a machine. Even the powder boys, climbing and descending the ladders in pitch-darkness, were carrying out their duties with exactitude, keeping the guns supplied with powder, for the guns never ceased from firing, bellowing in deafening fashion…."

—C.S. FORESTER
Hornblower and the "Hotspur"

Over a Barrel

One of the Royal Navy's nastiest and most common punishments was to strap a sailor across the barrel of one of the ship's guns for flogging. The phrase now applies to someone in a helpless predicament.

Overbearing

When a sailing ship with superior power came close to another boat and stole its wind it was said to be overbearing. Similarly, people who attempt to exert unwelcome control over others are considered overbearing.

Overboard

Anything that falls over the side of a boat. From Old English "bord," meaning board or plank. The expression now means to act or speak with excessive enthusiasm.

Squally weather, with rain. At 5 p.m. saw some sea weed pass the ship, and at 7 William Greenslade, marine, either by accident or design, went overboard and was drowned.

—CAPTAIN JAMES COOK
Journal During the First Voyage Round the World

Overhaul

The word overhaul held various meanings for sailors. Originally it described the process of setting the rigging by hauling on slack ropes run through pulleys. Eventually the word described inspection and repair of a ship. It may be used to describe one ship gaining on another. To overhaul a wardrobe, car, or tax code is to fix or improve it.

> When all the gear had been overhauled, and the Ross-shire was off with the wind on the beam, with everything drawing and the decks cleared up, all hands were called aft, and the watches were picked….
>
> —BASIL LUBBOCK
> *The Last of the Windjammers*

Overwhelm

When a ship founders or capsizes it is overwhelmed. From the Anglo-Saxon "whelmen," meaning to turn a ship completely over.

In a short time the fury of the wind and sea had been whipped up, and the "greybeards" which attempted to overtake us astern, with crests seemingly over a mile long, commenced to rear up, and at times we would see a tremendous green sea with a boiling whirlpool of foam on its crest approach as if to overwhelm us."

—CLAUDE WOOLLARD,
aboard the tall ship *Penrhyn Castle*

Pea Jacket

The name pea jacket, also known as a pea coat, comes from the Dutch word "pijjekker" meaning a coarse wool jacket. The pea jacket was originally worn in the 1800s by Dutch sailors. Later the British and US Navies adopted it. This sturdy, snug, double-breasted jacket with its wide flip-up collar protected sailors from wind and rain. It is now a classic that is both fashionable and functional.

> Going forward to the forecastle, we found the slide of the scuttle open. Seeing a light we went down, and found only an old rigger there, wrapped in a tattered pea-jacket.
>
> —Herman Melville
> *Moby Dick*

Pipe Down

During the day the boatswain piped different patterns of notes on his whistle to signal various orders. Silence and lights out were among the last commands of the day. Unlike voices that don't carry well at sea, the whistle's high-pitch could be heard above the wind, surf, and general din of the ship.

Pitch In

—⚓—

Sailors caulked the seams of the deck with hot tar pine called pitch. Caulking kept the deck watertight, preserved the wood, and added structural reinforcement. The crew had to pitch in to complete the task quickly while the tar was hot and malleable. Maintaining the deck was critical to the ship's integrity. As Thomas Gibbons once said, "There is but a plank between a sailor and eternity."

Point Blank

The phrase point blank is from Old French "point blanc," meaning the white bull's eye of a target. A ship's cannon shot fired at short-range travels in a straight line. Today it means blunt and direct speaking.

I had half a mind to ask him point-blank whether he, at least, didn't know why Falk, a notoriously unsociable man, had taken to visiting his ship with such assiduity.

—JOSEPH CONRAD
Falk: A Reminiscence

Pooped

The poop is the short, raised deck near the back of a ship. To be pooped is to be swamped by a heavy sea breaking over the stern. It is a potentially catastrophic event causing flooding, loss of momentum, and steerage. When we are pooped, we are likewise wiped out.

Posh

POSH is an acronym for "Port Outward, Starboard Home." Voyages from England to Colonial India were scorching hot. Well-to-do passengers avoided the baking sun by booking the desirable shaded staterooms on the port side of the ship heading out, and the starboard side returning. It's a colorful legend, but there has never been a ticket or document found stamped POSH. Nonetheless we still equate the word with things that are elegant, expensive, and luxurious.

Press into Service

—— ✸ ——

In seaports around the world, agents of the British Navy forced men into service. These unfortunate males received only a fraction of the regular crew pay. The practice of involuntary conscription ended in the mid 19th century when the Admiralty began offering enough pay to attract a sufficient number of volunteers.

Why in God's name did he ever come into the Navy? He was a volunteer, not a pressed man.

—Patrick O'Brian
Master and Commander

Press On

To press on means to work steadily towards a goal despite distractions or obstacles. The phrase comes from the idea of wind driving a ship forward by pressing against her sails. To maximize speed a captain might order as much setting of sail as possible. But caution was required. Straining a ship under full sail could result in costly and sometimes catastrophic damage to sails, rigging, and gear.

> The barque was storming along under fores'l and six top sails, the wind slightly quartering, so that every sail was bladder-hard and pulling its full weight.
>
> —Neil Campbell,
> aboard the four-masted barque *Elginshire*

Put through the Hoop

Rolled hammocks lashed to netting along the ship's railing were protection against shelling. Passing it through a cane hoop tested the tightness of the rolled hammock. A sailor with a sloppily folded hammock that did not fit through the hoop was reprimanded. When we undergo a rigorous challenge, we are put through the hoop.

Quarantine

All arriving ships, whether naval or commercial, posed a huge health threat to coastal cities. On the Mediterranean Sea, an approaching ship suspected of carrying infectious diseases was required to sit at anchor off-shore for forty days. The name of this waiting period comes from the Latin "Quadraesima," meaning "the forty days." The "quarantine flag," a solid yellow rectangle, was hoisted by ships approaching the harbor to warn that it carried contagions. Today the yellow flag has the opposite meaning: All on board are healthy and harbor clearance should be granted. The flag is lowered after customs formalities are completed.

Raining Cats and Dogs

In Norse mythology cats unleash rain and dogs stir up wind and storms. Odin, the Viking god of thunder, was frequently depicted with dogs and wolves. When the heavens opened up, seafarers held this Nordic deity of storms and his menagerie responsible.

Rats from a Sinking Ship

Sailors believed that rats deserting the ship signaled impending disaster. Indeed, rats are quick to detect trouble since they hide in places that often first take on water, such as a ship's hold or bilge.

> A rotten carcass of a butt, not rigg'd,
> Nor tackle, sail nor mast; the very rats
> instinctively had quit it.
>
> —WILLIAM SHAKESPEARE
> *The Tempest*

Rise and Shine

The order to rise and shine is a traditional morning call for the crew to wake-up, hit the deck, and be ready to take orders.

It was still dark next morning when I heard the boatswain's pipe and Morrison's call: 'All Hands! Turn out and save a clue! Out or down here! Out or down here! Rise and shine!'

—CHARLES NORDOFF AND JAMES NORMAN HALL

Mutiny on the Bounty

Round Robin

To hide the identity of the lead mutineer or instigator of a petition or complaint, British sailors signed their names in a circular form called a round robin. This clever ruse was adopted from France, where dissenting government officers wrote their names on a ribbon or sash attached at both ends. Robin is a corruption of the French word for ribbon, "ruban."

Rummage Sale

———— ✄ ————

Damaged, unclaimed, or unpaid for cargo was often peddled dockside to locals. The word rummage comes from the French "arrimage," meaning cargo in a ship's hold.

Run a Tight Ship

Taut rigging maximized sail power. Commands to adjust and keep the rigging tight had to be quickly executed by the crew. The phrase has come to describe an organization that is closely and efficiently managed.

Run the Gauntlet

Being forced to run the gauntlet was severe punishment for stealing meted out by the Royal Navy. Because crew members lived in such tight quarters, their possessions were easy targets for sailors with sticky fingers. If caught, the thief was forced to run between two rows of sailors who beat him with ropes.

Scuttle

———— ∞ ————

Ships could be sabotaged by cutting or boring holes in the hull below the waterline. In naval warfare, a captain facing certain defeat might order the ship scuttled to deprive the enemy of the spoils of victory and to avoid captivity. Scuttling was also an early form of insurance fraud. Dishonest sea merchants grossly inflated the value of their vessels and cargo, sank them, and then collected.

Scuttlebutt

A "butt" was a large wooden drinking water cask where sailors gathered around and swapped rumors and stories. On long voyages, water was rationed by carving a hole in the cask's side so that it could only be half filled. A cask with a hole was "scuttled." Not much has changed except we now gossip around a water cooler.

Shipshape

To function smoothly, sailing vessels must have every-thing in its proper place. A crew executes commands quickly and efficiently when gear and rigging are orderly and neat.

After a day of strenuous toil by all hands, we suc-ceeded in getting things a bit ship-shape once more....The decks were clear of ice, and tempo-rary patches of canvas and timber nailed over where the ice had broken right through.

—Percy Allen Eaddy
Hull Down

Shot across the Bow

In the 18th century, navies forced oncoming ships to identify themselves by firing a cannon shot over their bow. If
the approaching ship hoisted enemy colors an attack might
ensue. Traditionally warships had the right to disguise
themselves by sailing under neutral or false flags, but once
they went into battle they were required to fly their country's true colors.

Shove Off

To shove off is to push a boat away from the shore, wharf, or hull of the main ship and out onto the water. Now slang for telling someone to get lost or go away.

Show a Leg

Under King George III, men were forced to serve in the navy against their will. To minimize desertions on long voyages, some sailors were permitted to bring their wives. Having women bunking among the crew created confusion during morning call. The problem was solved by wives draping a leg over the edge of the bunk as a signal to the officer to leave them in peace.

Show the Flag

Maritime law required all ships to display the flag of its country of origin. Flags served to identify a hostile ship or one from a plague-ridden country. As symbols of power, national flags were used to stake claims in foreign waters. It has come to mean showing up in support of someone or some cause.

Shrouds

To support the mast, heavy ropes called shrouds were extended from the masthead and secured to the ship's sides. So many were required to do the job that they partially obscured the mast, giving it the appearance of being cloaked. Shrouds eventually took on the general meaning of coverings and burial garments. According to his wishes, Lord Nelson was laid to rest inside the mast of the warship he had destroyed in the Battle of the Nile. As such, the mast of the *L'Orient* warship shrouded him at his funeral.

…. I started up the topmast shrouds half afraid of it, as if it might pursue me. The topmast shrouds were secured to the top with bottle-screws…. Once or twice I was tempted to look down, I was overcome with vertigo.

—FRANK BAINES, voyage on the tall ship *Lawhill*

Sick Bay

The original floating infirmary was located in the lower
deck of the ship's rounded stern. The curved shape of
the stern suggested a bay and so sailors began calling
it the sick bay. Equipped with a medicine chest and berths,
the sick bays were gloomy, stuffy, and cramped—not ideal
conditions for convalescing.

> From the situation of the bay, then, it is necessarily
> exposed to the damp air of the cable-tier, as well as
> the cold air of the mid-hatch above it, which is gen-
> erally open, as its after end; and to the unpleasant
> smell of the fore-hold, where the beef, pork, &c.
> are kept ….Can any place, then, be conceived of,
> better calculated to injure patients and distress the
> surgeon, then such a sick-bay.
>
> —WILLIAM P. C. BARTON, US Naval Surgeon
>
> *A Treatise Containing a Plan for the Internal Organization
> and Government of Marine Hospitals in the United States,*
> 1814

Skyscraper

The skyscraper was the highest sail on a tall ship. These small triangular sails were made of light cloth and only used in fair winds. Sky sails were set just below the skyscraper.

The yankee clipper is under her skysails,
She cuts the sparkle and scud,
My eyes settle the land, I bend at her
prow or shout joyously from the deck.

—Walt Whitman
Leaves of Grass

Sloppy

Sloppy comes from the Middle English word "sloppe," meaning baggy outerwear. British Navy recruits were so shabbily dressed in their patched, threadbare clothing, that even the low quality garments they eventually bought from the ship's store were a step up. Their most common purchase was the ubiquitous baggy pants called "slops." The disheveled British sailor was given a makeover in 1857 when the Royal Navy rolled out official uniforms.

Slush Fund

Fatty scraps from boiling meat were collected by the ship cooks. The fat was intended for use by the crew to prevent chafing and rot in the rigging, but often these poorly paid cooks kept the fatty slush hidden and sold it to candle makers back in port. Today's political slush funds are similar—they are hidden and they stink.

Smoke Screen

By decreasing the amount of air supply to combustion engines, 19th century naval ships could release thick, oily smoke that lay over the water for hours. The smoke hid the ship's maneuvers from the enemy. The term is now used more broadly to describe something said or done to obscure, confuse, or hide the truth.

Snub

To snub was to abruptly halt a vessel by dropping anchor or by securing a running line by tying it to a post or cleat. Nowadays to snub is to rebuff or keep someone in check with a curt or disdainful remark.

The little ship, almost empty of stores was the plaything of wind and wave and tide: she surged about at her anchors like a restive horse. She swung and she snubbed herself steady with a jerk; she plunged and snubbed herself again.

—C. S. FORESTER
Hornblower and the "Hotspur"

Son of a Gun

Some British warships allowed women on board, with obvious consequences. Since sailors had no privacy below deck, babies were often conceived and delivered in the relatively secluded spaces between the ship's guns. When paternity was unknown, the child was entered in the ship's log as "son of a gun."

> The surgeon informed me that a woman on board had been laboring for twelve hours, and if I could permit the firing of a broadside nature would be assisted by the shock. I complied and she was delivered of a fine male child.
>
> —Captain W. N. Glascock
> *Diary entry, 1835*

SOS

Early 20th century transatlantic ships could telegraph distress by tapping out Morse code signals heard in telegraph stations on both sides of the Atlantic. A distinct combination of sounds: three dots, three dashes, and three dots, represented the letters SOS (...— — —...) The dash sounded three times as long as the dot.

Spick and Span

Spick and span described a newly constructed wooden ship. A spick was a nail or spike, and a span was a piece of wood cut from timber. The phrase has come to mean anything that is tidy and spotless. In 1933 two Michigan housewives dropped the "k" and adopted the name for their hugely popular household cleaner "Spic and Span."

Square Meal

At anchor or in fair weather, sailors were served meals on square wooden boards. The square shape made for easy stacking and stowing. In rough weather the busy crew simply ate whatever food they could stash in their pockets.

Squared Away

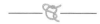

On square-rigger ships, horizontal wooden spars were attached to the mast. These spars are called yards. Sails were set from these yards. When sailing with the wind, the yards were positioned at right angles to the deck to best catch the wind. Squared away now means to put things in order or a state of readiness.

A lively breeze sprang up. 'Square away the yards!' ordered the Captain, from the poop. All hands tailed on the braces, and soon the barque was slipping through the water, with everything drawing.

— Sir James Bisset
Sail Ho!

Standoffish

When a ship approaches a port but delays entry due to unsafe conditions, she will tack toward and away from the entrance in a holding pattern. These days, standoffish is to keep one's distance.

Strike

Poor conditions and low, infrequent pay fueled sailors' resentments. Since mutiny was a high-risk proposition and desertion impossible at sea, disgruntled crew members protested in ports. Work slowdowns included immobilizing the ship by hauling down (striking) its sails. The word "strike" was later adopted by other working groups.

Taken Aback

A ship is pushed backward when violent winds or a careless helmsman cause the sails to blow rearward against the mast. This sudden predicament could snap the mast or severely damage the rigging. As a figure of speech, taken aback means to be astonished by some unwelcome occurrence.

> Luckily, we were not taken aback, or the three sticks and all they carried aloft would have been over the side, or the ship on her beam ends with the cargo shifted.

> —ELIS KARLSSON
> *Pully-Haul: The Story of a Voyage*

Taken Down a Peg

For centuries, the position of naval flags on the ships' masts indicated rank. The flag of a senior admiral flew high on the main mast. When the admiral handed over command to his junior, the flag halyard, which was secured by pegs, would be lowered, or taken down a peg. Today the expression means to deflate or humble someone.

Take the Wind Out of Your Sails

A maneuver by which one boat passes windward and close to another boat, so as to block the breeze from the other's sails. It is humiliating for captains to lose speed and have their sails sag. The phrase now means to make someone less boastful. The egomaniacal politician had the wind taken out of his sails when his opponent won by a landslide.

Tattoo

The Tahitian word "tatau," meaning to mark was adopted by Captain James Cook and his men during their exploration of the South Seas in the 1700s. Inspired by the Polynesian body art, Cook's crew returned home with tattoos. These were not the first sailors to be inked. For centuries seamen were exposed to cultures that decorated their skin with imbedded substances. Sailors are superstitious and many nautical tattoos are good luck talismans: the anchor for stability and strength, the North Star and compass rose for safe navigation, and the migratory swallow to ensure a return home.

> At other times, one of the tattooing artists would crawl over the bulwarks followed by his sitter, and then a bare arm or leg would be extended, and the disagreeable business of "pricking" commence, right under my eyes….
>
> —HERMAN MELVILLE
> *White-Jacket*

The Three-Mile Limit

According to international law, a country's territorial waters extend three miles beyond its coastline. Why three miles? When this maritime act was established in the late 18th century, a nation's practical ability to control its waters was limited to the maximum three-mile trajectory of the most powerful cannons of the time.

> The dominion of the land ends where the power of the arms end.
>
> —CORNELIUS VAN BYNKERSHOEK,
> Dutch jurist

Three Sheets to the Wind

The expression three sheets to the wind stems from the similarity between a drunken sailor staggering about, and a sailing ship moving erratically because its sheets are flying loose in the wind.

> Maybe you think we were all a sheet in the wind's eye. But I'll tell you I was sober.

—ROBERT LOUIS STEVENSON
Treasure Island

Tide Over

—— ✺ ——

To tide over was the technique of alternating between sailing and anchoring when battling headwinds and unfavorable tides. This allowed a boat to hold its position until conditions improved. The term now describes enabling someone to get through a difficult period, most commonly by lending money.

Ties That Bind

A short, sturdy chain tightly bound the support rigging to the ship's mast. The expression has come to describe the close bonds formed by blood relations, shared experiences, or common beliefs.

> David Jones was married to Anne Robinson. They had been old shipmates on board the Le Seine where the lady bore a conspicuous part in the different actions in which the frigate was engaged…. An attachment took place which ended in their union.
>
> —A *London Journal* marriage announcement, 1802

Toe the Line

When commanding the crew to come to attention, the captain expected uniformity and precision. Sailors lined up with their toes touching the seams of the planking. A sailor not standing upright and in proper alignment was ordered to toe the line.

Tonnage

Because wine was an important cargo, by the 13th century a ship's size was measured by the number of wine casks in the hold. A wine cask was called a "tun" from the French word for cask. A duty was levied on each tun of wine imported. Eventually tonnage denoted total weight in tons shipped.

> Posted missing. The barque Vitula, five hundred tons. New York to Melbourne overdue and presumed lost.
>
> —Lloyd's of London

Touch and Go

A ship scraping bottom lightly and quickly with no damage to the keel and little loss of speed is said to touch and go. It has come to mean a precarious situation with an uncertain outcome.

> It was touch and go; only a few yards separated the two vessels, when there was a clatter of bells aboard the steamer and she swerved sharply to port.
>
> —REX CLEMENT, aboard the frigate HMS *Arethusa*

True Blue

Coventry, England, was renowned for producing a high quality, colorfast blue wool. Gradually true blue became synonymous with the Royal Navy's reputation for steadfast loyalty to the Crown.

True Colors

The colors of a ship's flag indicated her nationality. The Royal Navy's Articles of War required its warships to fly the British flag when entering battle, but admirals often wanted to trick the enemy by flying flags of false colors. By waiting until the very last moment to hoist their true colors they could fool the foe *and* obey the law.

At 1.50, having closed with the enemy to about two miles, he shortened sail to his topgallant sails, jib, and spanker, and luff'd up to the wind; hoisted our colours, and put ourselves under the same sail, and bore down on him…at 2.10 when a half mile distant, he opened his fire…

—*The Naval Chronicle*, report on the capture of the HMS *Java* by the USS *Constitution*

Turn a Blind Eye

In one of naval history's most celebrated acts of insubordination in the heat of battle, Admiral Nelson raised his telescope to his blind eye and announced he could not see the signal flag commanding him to break off action. As the story goes, Nelson told his captain, "You know Foley I have only one eye, and I have a right to be blind sometimes." Since Nelson pulled off a spectacular victory, naval superiors naturally turned a blind eye to his disobedience.

Under the Weather

A sailor standing watch on the windward side of the ship is battered by wind and spray. Getting the brunt of the rough seas he or she was said to be under the weather.

Under Your Own Steam

In their early days, steamships were prone to boiler room explosions. If one arrived at port without incident it was a success. The expression now means to accomplish something without assistance.

Walk the Plank

Sailors, and most famously pirates, extended a plank off the ship's side and forced their victims to walk to the end, plunging into the sea. While the practice is gone, the lore remains. Nowadays it's a metaphor for having to submit to consequences beyond one's control. Images of walking the plank are found in Hollywood films, and the works of Robert Louis Stevenson and Mark Twain.

> Oh, they just have a bully time—take ships and burn them, and get the money and bury it in awful places in their island where there's ghosts and things to watch it, and kill everybody in the ships—make 'em walk a plank.
>
> —Mark Twain
> *The Adventures of Tom Sawyer*

Wallop

After the French torched the English coastal town of Brighton, Henry VIII ordered the English Admiral Wallop to retaliate. He did so with a vengeance—burning French ships and destroying French villages on the Normandy coast. The name Wallop became synonymous with a hard hit. The hurricane walloped the coastline.

Washed Out

Naval commands were written on a slate. Once received by the crew, the message was washed off the board. It's a term that's become synonymous with someone or something that is a total failure.

When Your Ship Comes In

After supplying a ship, hiring crew, and paying insurance and port dues, merchants watched this vast investment vanish over the horizon for months or years. The lucky financier reaped huge profits when his ship returned with precious cargo. Unlucky investors waited for a ship that never reappeared. Today the expression has a more metaphorical meaning—a hope that one's fortunes will someday change for the better.

Ships at a distance have every man's wish on board. For some they come in with the tide. For others they sail forever on the horizon, never out of sight, never landing until the Watcher turns his eyes away in resignation, his dreams mocked to death by Time. That is the life of men.

—Zora Neale Hurston
Their Eyes Were Watching God

Whistle for the Wind

When a ship was becalmed it was the seaman's superstition that he could summon the wind by facing the direction from which he desired the wind to blow, and whistling. Nowadays to be whistling in the wind is a futile attempt to change something unalterable.

Windfall

For naval ship building purposes, the British monarchy could lay claim to trees on private property. There was an exception to this law; if the wind caused a tree to fall, the landowner could keep the tree for his own use or sell it for profit, a windfall.

You Scratch My Back, I'll Scratch Yours

One of the British Royal Navy's preferred instruments of corporal punishment was the cat-o'-nine tails. This nasty whip with nine varying lengths of knotted cord was designed to claw deeply into a sailor's back. Mindful that what goes around can come around, some sailors charged with doing the lashing applied only light strikes that amounted to little more than a scratch on the back.

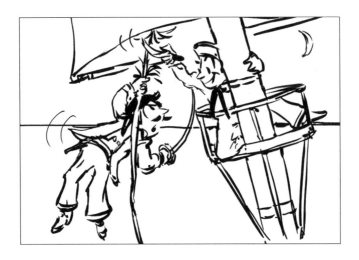

Your Number Is Up

An admiral needing to confer with or reprimand one of the captains in his fleet summoned him by flying the number of that ship. Hence the captain's number was up. The phrase now implies that it is someone's turn for death or bad fortune.

Acknowledgments

I am grateful to friends for their sustained enthusiasm and support for the book, including Elissa Altman, Bob Bellafronto, Peter Bertine, Chris Cunningham, Jeannine Dillon, Linda Doering, Stefan Dziemianowicz, Mimi Fahs, Rachel Federman, Carolyn Jaffe, Brian Jaffe, Diana Jagannath, Vilas Jagannath, Carol Jaspin, Terry Karten, Anne Keating, Rama Rao, Sarah Salm, Nancy Shapiro, Elly Thomas, and Judy Willard. My sister Sandra has been wonderfully enthusiastic since I first shared with her the idea for *Three Sheets to the Wind*. I'm very fortunate to have my brother Vail joined in the project and enrich it with his illustrations. Susi, my wife, added a keen editorial eye and sense of fun to the project. Many thanks go to Vanessa Cameron and the New York Yacht Club for providing me with access to their magnificent maritime library. My longtime friend and colleague, Shaye Areheart, Director of the Columbia Publishing Course, has been a terrific advocate for the book from the moment I told her about it. Laura Barr's artistic and technological talents have been a great help in launching *Three Sheets to the Wind*. I am very grateful to my agent and friend Malaga Baldi. She has been positive and supportive every step of the way. Susan Turner, the designer, found just the right look for the interior and it's been a pleasure working with her. I'm fortunate to have Rick Rinehart at Lyons Press as my editor. He shares my love of sailing and the language of the sea. Thanks also to Diana Nuhn for the cover design, Lynn Zelem for her careful review of the text, and to the rest of the staff at Lyons Press.

About the Author

CYNTHIA BARRETT is a senior editor at Metro Books, an imprint of Sterling Publishing Company. She is an avid sailor and has a long family history near the sea. She lives with her wife, Susi Vassallo, in New York City.

About the Illustrator

VAIL BARRETT is a painter and illustrator. His works have shown in galleries in New England, New Jersey, and New York. He lives in Roxbury, Connecticut.